50

WAYS YOU CAN HELP

SAVE the

PLANET

Tony Campolo
& Gordon Aeschliman

INTERVARSITY PRESS
DOWNERS GROVE, ILLINOIS 6051

InterVarsity Press is the book-publishing division of InterVarsity Christian Fellowship, a student movement active on campus at hundreds of universities, colleges and schools of nursing in the United States of America, and a member movement of the International Fellowship of Evangelical Students. For information about local and regional activities, write Public Relations Dept., InterVarsity Christian Fellowship, 6400 Schroeder Rd., P.O. Box 7895, Madison, WI 53707-7895.

All Scripture quotations, unless otherwise indicated, are taken from the HOLY BIBLE, NEW INTERNATIONAL VERSION. Copyright © 1973, 1978, 1984 International Bible Society. Used by permission of Zondervan Publishing House. All rights reserved.

Cover illustration: Paul Turnbaugh

Printed on recycled paper.

ISBN 0-8308-1392-6

Printed in the United States of America

Library of Congress Cataloging-in-Publication Data

Aeschliman, Gordon D., 1957-
    50 ways you can help save the planet/by Gordon Aeschliman and Tony Campolo.
      p.   cm.
    ISBN 0-8308-1392-6
    1. Environmental protection—Citizen participation.
    2. Conservation of natural resources—Citizen participation.
    3. Stewardship, Christian.   I. Campolo, Anthony.   II. Title.
    III. Title: Fifty ways you can help save the planet.
    TD171.7.A47   1992
    363.7'0525—dc20   91-46005
                                           CIP

15	14	13	12	11	10	9	8	7	6	5	4	3	2	1
03	02	01	00	99	98	97	96	95	94	93	92			

For the Love of Creation . . . ———————————— **9**

I. Recycle ———————————————————————— **15**

  1. Paper Chase: At Home ——————————————— **19**

  2. Paper Chase: At the Office ————————————— **23**

  3. Well Oiled —————————————————————— **25**

  4. The Plastic People ———————————————— **27**

  5. Go for the Metal ————————————————— **29**

  6. Get Some Glass! ————————————————— **31**

  7. Catch the Contaminants ————————————— **33**

  8. Stamp Out Styrofoam —————————————— **35**

  9. Get a Charge ——————————————————— **37**

  10. Hand-Me-Downs ————————————————— **39**

  11. Gray the Garden ————————————————— **41**

  12. Precycle ————————————————————— **43**

  13. Reduced Use Zone Ahead ———————————— **45**

  14. Adopt-a-Block —————————————————— **47**

  15. Adopt-an-Office ————————————————— **49**

  16. Adopt-a-Road —————————————————— **51**

  17. Convert Your Church ——————————————— **53**

  18. Clean Sweep ——————————————————— **55**

  19. Elderly Aid ————————————————————— **57**

  20. Start Your Own Company ————————————— **59**

II. Water —————————————————————————— **61**

  21. Check the Flow —————————————————— **65**

  22. Reduce the Flow: Indoors ———————————— **67**

23. Reduce the Flow: Outdoors ——————— 69

24. Keep It Clean ——————————————— 71

25. Make a Career of It ———————————— 73

III. Energy ———————————————————— 75

26. Go Natural ——————————————————— 79

27. Patch the Leaks ———————————————— 82

28. Step in Line ——————————————————— 84

29. Go Lite on Lights ———————————————— 86

30. Watch Those Appliances ——————————— 88

IV. Shop Green ——————————————————— 91

31. Green Gifts ————————————————————— 94

32. Buy Local ————————————————————— 96

33. Look for the Labels ———————————————— 98

34. Buying Big ————————————————————— 100

35. Boycott Buying ————————————————— 102

V. The Garden of Eden ——————————————— 103

36. ReLeaf ———————————————————————— 106

37. ReLeaf at Christmas ——————————————— 109

38. A Bird in the . . . ———————————————————— 111

39. Green Thumb It ———————————————————— 113

40. Don't Be a Dodo ——————————————————— 115

VI. Advocate ——————————————————————— 117

41. Celebrate Earth Day ——————————————— 120

42. Educate ——————————————————————— 122

43. Write the Wrong ———————————————————— 124

44. Mark Your "X" —————————————————————— 127

45. Make a Scene ———————————————————————— 129

VII. Resources for Action ———————————————— 131

46. Magazines ———————————————————————————— 134

47. Books ———————————————————————————————— 135

48. Federal Agencies and Offices ————————————— 136

49. State Recycling Agencies ——————————————— 138

50. National Organizations —————————————————— 145

For the
Love
of Creation . . .

Confusion, fuzzy thinking and unfriendly name calling
surround the Christian community's debate on our responsibility to the environment. This book is not a part of that debate.

Our goal, quite simply, has been to assemble fifty practical
ways in which Christians can actually make a difference in saving the planet God has given to us. Our approach in the pages
that follow is upbeat and optimistic. We want to encourage
Christians whose relationship with Christ has led them to a
sensitive concern for creation.

Having said that, we think it is important for those activists
who use this handy manual to understand some of our motiva-
tions in publishing it.

Return to Eden?

Two extremes emerge in the debate regarding the environment. One group appears to be motivated by a vision to return this planet to the pristine conditions that existed prior to the Fall—a sort of utopian garden.

We are not motivated by this vision. All of Scripture and history point to the fact that we cannot return to Eden. Our entire human condition is cursed by the Fall, and that includes creation, which, according to the Bible, groans in anticipation of its day of redemption.

The other extreme position in the debate among Christians is that the world is essentially "going to hell in a handbasket." Prophecy tells of the final destructive war, cataclysmic earthquakes and red moon, so why try to rescue something that is only going to get worse? If you can't fix it, why put Band-aids on it?

Obviously, we are not motivated by this form of thinking either. We would simply point out a parallel.

Christians share the gospel message with many people, even though they know that probably only a few will respond. In the same way, Christians ought to be willing to care for the created world, even though they know that full restoration is not possible. We obey God because he is God, not because he promises us success.

Creation Affirms God's Authority

One reason we are motivated to care for the environment is that it is an awesome display of God's final authority over all of life. God created all there is. As the author of Colossians tells us: "For by him all things were created: things in heaven and on earth, visible and invisible . . . all things were created by him and for him. He is before all things, and in him all things hold together" (Col 1:16-17).

As we tend the garden we are acknowledging the rule of a higher authority over all of life. During our most severe trials and sufferings, when painful questions weigh upon our emotions and lead us to doubt the existence of an all-powerful God who is ready to come to our rescue, we can turn to creation for reassurance and courage. God did this for Job in his darkest hour. Job 38—41 is the Bible's best case for showing that creation points to the sovereign Lord. We quote just a few verses from the beginning (38:4-6):

Where were you when I laid the earth's foundation?
Tell me, if you understand.
Who marked off its dimensions?
   Surely you know!
Who stretched a measuring line across it?
On what were its footings set, or who laid its cornerstone?

Creation Worships God

The Scripture tells us that were we to silence our praises to God, all creation, including such inanimate objects as rocks, would burst forth in audible praise. Indeed, the silent praise of flowers in spring, blooming trees and schools of magnificent fluorescent fish tells the glories of an awesome Creator. And the near-overwhelming chorus of adulation from jungle creatures in the early hours of the morning renders our best choral attempts at praise insignificant. We go to the environment to listen to its worship

11

of our heavenly Father, and we care to preserve it from destruction so that we can regularly return to be ministered to by its songs of adoration.

Creation Leads People to God

The heavens display the wonders of God. Creation speaks of the One who holds all eternity in his hands.

Religious people have, since the beginning of time, been drawn to discover a personal God through his fingerprints on creation. This relentless search, which expresses the continual and ultimate aspirations of the human race, is in fact spurred on by the voice of nature, the masterpiece of God's handiwork. When we stand back to appreciate a painting or sculpture of a Renaissance artist, we are drawn to wonder at the superior gift. And these masterworks pale in comparison to the ultimate work of art, the created world. We are motivated to preserve this display of God.

Our Worship and Witness

Every small deed of tending the garden is an act of worship. It is our bowed knee to the One who created the garden and calls us to live in it. We show by our care of the environment that we respect God's detailed work of living art.

And the converse is also true. When we mindlessly and perhaps arrogantly crush fellow creatures beneath our materialistic advances, we are demonstrating blatant disregard for our Creator. We are making an unequivocal statement that we do not regard highly the One who breathed and continues to breathe life into creation.

Another thing: Our worship of God, displayed in our respect and care for the garden, is a witness to the people of the world. It is a witness because we are saying that we have found a personal relationship with the Creator. We have come to understand that the marvelous hand of God not only stretches a canopy of stars across the heavens each night but also reaches down to hold our hand. By our act of creation care, we are building a bridge to those who *do* glory in creation but are not sure that it points to a Supreme Being just within reach. They hope it does. If they could only find out how to join hands with the loving Creator!

This is our supreme joy and privilege. It is our opinion that Christians who stamp out creation in arrogant disregard are working *against* the task of evangelism, putting in place stumbling blocks for people whose respect of creation rejects a Christian answer to finding God because of apparent Christian disregard for creation.

And we would add: Our destruction of the environment is a statement that we do not hold hope that God will remain patient in his return to allow more to come into salvation before that final hour of reckoning.

Ultimately, our care of creation is motivated by a deep love for Jesus. First, our taking care of the garden is an act of gratitude for the One who planted the trees and flowers and placed the birds, animals and fish for our delight and sustenance in this life. Second, we are forever grateful for the freedom we have received in the forgiveness of our sins, the gift of the Holy Spirit and the hope of living forever in a new world where there will be no destruction or decay.

We sincerely hope that this book will help you in your acts of worship and love. We trust that these fifty practical ideas will lead you deeper in your journey of faith and love. And we are convinced that this concrete form of obedience and witness to the Lord will help bring about both a harvest—of people turning to God and growing in him—and a garden of refreshment which will bring delight both to earth's people and to the Creator.

Do you have any ideas, resources or agencies you'd like to see included in a possible future edition of 50 Ways You Can Help Save the Planet? *If so, send them to Gordon Aeschliman, P.O. Box 25, Colfax, WA 99111. We'd love to hear from you.*

I

Recycle

● ● ● ● ● ● ● ● ● ● ● ● ● ● ●

Recycling is the simplest and perhaps the most important way we can care for the environment. The good news is that everyone can take part in this effort—and can really make a difference. The bad news . . . there *is* no bad news.

We will suggest twenty ways you or your group can recycle. We recommend that you read through the entire section and then choose five or six ideas that you can realistically implement. Every bit makes a difference, so it doesn't make sense to overload and then give up.

There are several good reasons to recycle.

The first reason is *waste*. Every time we throw away something, it has to be replaced. The cost of replacement is enormous. For example, Americans throw away 500,000 trees every week—trees that could have been saved if we recycled our newspapers. That means replacement costs us a large forest, all the resources (such as fuel) which were used up in cutting and processing those trees, and all the clean air that was polluted by diesel tractors and trucks involved in the deforestation. *Every week.*

It costs 65 per cent more *energy* to make one ton of new paper than it costs to make one ton of recycled paper. It costs 7,000 gallons more *water* to make that same ton of new paper than it would have cost to make a ton of recycled paper. And a ton of paper can be recycled up to seven times.

It costs to throw away (and therefore replace) metal. Every year, Americans discard enough aluminum to replace the nation's entire commercial air fleet four times. Similarly, we throw away enough iron and steel to supply all the nation's auto makers—continuously. According to the EarthWorks Group, it takes four times as much energy to make steel from virgin ore as it does to make the same amount of steel from scrap. And as you might guess, it costs equally exorbitant amounts to replace other materials such as plastics and glass.

A second good reason to recycle is *pollution*. When the garbage trucks disappear down the road with our trash, the garbage may be out of our sight, but it is not out of our system. There is no pollution-free method of disposal. Carting away the trash belches tons of exhaust into the air (approximately 360,000 trucks make the journey to the dumps six times each day in the U.S.); rotting garbage in landfills releases toxic gases; chemicals from garbage seep into the underground water system and end up in our vegetables, fruits and faucets.

Here's a way to visualize the size of the problem: There are fewer churches in America than garbage trucks, and fewer full-time Christian workers than full-time garbage haulers.

A third good reason to recycle is *personal.* It is our lifestyle that creates all the garbage and pollution, so in response it is our lifestyle that brings about correctives. Caring for the environment is a reflection of our worship of God the Creator. For this reason, each act of recycling is a form of spiritual worship. It is our personal relationship to God being expressed in tangible terms.

1
Paper Chase: At Home

· · · · · · · · · · · ·

The single greatest contributor to waste is paper. In fact, as much as 40 per cent of America's garbage is paper. Recycling paper is a relatively simple task and yet has enormous value for creation. The most seasoned environmentalists have incorporated recycling paper into their very lifestyle, and to them it is as natural a daily routine as brushing teeth. This could easily be true for all of us. We've listed a few categories for implementation:

Newspapers
Most Americans get a newspaper, be it daily or on weekends, and every day we throw away 42 million of them. Create a newspaper box in a convenient location that is dry, away from the wind and

easy to get to (encourage the habit by making it easy on yourself and your household). Don't allow yourself to read the next day's paper until the previous one is in the recycle box.

If your community doesn't yet have curbside pickup of newspapers, then once a week (or whenever the bin is full) include a stop at your town's recycling center when doing other regular errands. Or consider supporting a youth club or some other organization that sells newspapers for recycling. Look up the Boy Scouts or other worthwhile groups in the phone book to locate their dropoff centers.

Many large newspaper corporations are now printing on recycled newspaper. The *Los Angeles Times,* this nation's largest metropolitan newspaper, uses 60 per cent recycled paper. Because newsprint is easily recycled, you might be reading fresh news on old paper that has gone through seven editions!

Cardboard

Recycling plants love cardboard. Divide your cardboard waste into two groups: glossy (for example, cereal boxes, small appliance boxes) and regular (U-Haul boxes, packing dividers, egg cartons and the like). Glossy cardboard has limited uses and, because of the special finish on it, must go through a special recycling process. It ends up in the same sorts of packages once again—cereal boxes and the like. Regular cardboard will go through several generations of recycling and will show up in any cardboard product. You will be surprised to discover how much cardboard goes through your house. Keep the two recycle boxes near the newspaper bin, and make the trip to the recycling center whenever they begin to overflow.

Magazines

Magazines are coated with a glossy substance that bars them from being recycled with newspapers (as much as 70 per cent of a magazine's weight is due to the gloss). If you are already recycling glossy cardboard, then you're set for magazines—they probably go in the same box. (The folks at your recycling center can tell you how they prefer materials sorted.) You may one day hold part of your *Time* magazine in the form of a Cheerios box.

Bags

Those brown paper grocery bags are big culprits in regard to the environment. If all of our grocery bags were used just twice, rather than once, Americans would save 1.5 million trees per year. Our suggestion is simple. Once you've unpacked the groceries in the kitchen, fold all the bags into one bag and put them in your trunk. The next time you go shopping they'll be going with you. Hand them to the checkout clerk when you're ready to pay. Most stores are environmentally conscious enough to oblige happily, and besides, you're saving them money. Keep up this routine as long as the bags last, and then recycle them with your regular cardboard. Start the process over on the next shopping trip.

Speaking of bags, many stores are now accepting the plastic grocery bags back. Stuff several into one, then drop them in the store's plastic recycle bin on your next trip.

Other

Paper towels, message pads, junk mail, class notes . . . the list doesn't end. Keep a box for these miscellaneous items. Check with your recycling center ahead of time to see what guidelines it has for sorting "all the rest." For sure you will need to remove the adhesive labels from junk mail and the plastic windows from envelopes before they make it into the recycle bin. Envelopes may not be recyclable because of the glue on them.

2
Paper Chase: At the Office

· · · · · · · · · · · · ·

If you have discovered the volume of paper waste at your home, you will be amazed to find how much paper corporate America throws into the bin. The EarthWorks Group provides a graphic picture: Americans discard enough office paper each year to build a twelve-foot wall all the way from California to New York.

If you are employed outside the home, we recommend that you take leadership at your office to implement a recycling system similar to the one you create at home. You'll need to use your creativity—for example, color-coded boxes strategically located throughout the office for specific types of paper waste. A wastebasket next to each desk is an invitation for waste. One suggestion you could make is to provide fashionable recycle trays in place of wastebaskets and put the wastebaskets in a location where you have to move away from the desk in order to throw things away. Always make recycling easier than disposal.

Volunteer to empty the recycle bins and deliver the paper to a recycling center. If the center pays for paper, you may want to spend it on an office treat, or the office may decide to donate all its paper to a charitable organization such as the Girl Scouts. You could *double* your recycling effort by donating all the money to an environmental organization.

One suggestion for the office concerns the *type* of paper your company purchases. Colored paper always costs more to recycle than white paper. See if you can influence your purchasing department away from items such as yellow note pads, pink message slips and colored copying paper. Be aware, too, that many types of recycled office paper products are now available.

3
Well Oiled

· · · · · · · · · · · · ·

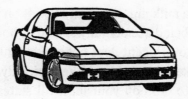

Used to be, every six months or so, dads across America would scoot under their cars and pickups and drain the dirty oil. Discarding the sludge was no problem—it went down the storm drain.

Thankfully, we know better now, and few dads would want to be caught in the act. We have learned that discarded oil makes its way into the rivers, lakes and oceans, destroying plants, fish and insects. Besides the damage to the environment, improperly discarded oil can hurt us: One quart of motor oil contaminates 250,000 gallons of drinking water. According to several environmental watch groups, Americans currently throw away the equivalent of 120 supertankers full of oil each year. Corporately, we are guilty of much greater oil abuse than the Exxon Valdez spill.

Changing the oil in our cars is important to the environment. Engines run better and last longer on clean oil. So keep changing the oil; just be sure to recycle. If you change your own oil, contact your local city government to see whether it accepts used oil. Many cities use discarded oil to heat city-owned buildings. Some city dumps will accept used oil and ship it in bulk to companies that recycle. If this is the case in your town, put your used oil in a milk jug, seal it and take it on your next errand run to avoid its being accidentally spilled at home.

If your local government does not provide this service, a local gas station is likely to recycle. Make a friendly contact first, to find out where to drop off your jugs. All states are required to make provisions for toxic waste, so call your state government if all else fails.

If you have your oil changed by a service station, be sure to inquire ahead of time whether it recycles. If not, find one that does. It's your oil, so don't leave the responsibility in someone else's hands.

One final suggestion: If you work at a gas station, a power plant or some other business that regularly changes oil, find out what the company's recycling procedures are. If none are in place, volunteer your cheerful services.

4

The Plastic People

· · · · · · · · · · · ·

Some have labeled us a plastic society because of our
use of "plastic money"—the credit card. We are actually more
plastic in our consumption than we realize. Here are a few
statistics we've assembled from various magazines and books:

☐ 98 per cent of all heavy jugs (milk, oil, bleach) are thrown
away.

☐ 98 per cent of all packaging (yogurt containers, pop lids) is
thrown away.

☐ U.S. citizens use 2.5 million bottles per hour.

☐ Basically *no* low-density plastic (sandwich bags, shrink-wrap
covers, vegetable bags) is recycled.

☐ 0.01 per cent of PVC plastic (used in plumbing) is recycled.

☐ 30 per cent of PET plastic (pop bottles, peanut butter jars) is recycled. Our best accomplishment.

☐ One-third of all carpets are made from recycled PET bottles.

☐ 26 recycled PET bottles make one polyester suit.

To begin recycling plastic, first contact your local recycling center to find out how it should be delivered. Some want you to sort according to the number inside the "recycle triangle." Some are happy to do the sorting if you do them the favor of cleaning out the containers. Organize your home recycling center to accommodate your plastic lifestyle.

As with paper, take the lead at your office in recycling plastics. Certain industries, of course, use more plastics so you will be taking on a substantial task. Get one or more co-workers to team up with you. You can do simple things like putting a box next to the lunchroom door, clearly marked Recycle Plastic Bottles Here—Thanks! Again, there can be financial rewards from recycling centers.

You may wonder where all that recycled material ends up. Most of it is "downgraded"—that is, re-formed into a use that does not involve food. The sensible precaution here is to prevent contaminated plastic from ending up as your next jug of milk. At a recycling plant, plastic is sorted according to type and then ground super-fine before being reused. It shows up in nonfood containers, carpets, ski jackets, rope and upholstery, to name a few destinations.

5

Go for the Metal

We use several types of metal each day. The most common is aluminum cans—the type that holds most of our soft drinks. Americans are great at recycling these. Already more than 60 per cent of these cans make it to recycling centers. Every time an aluminum can is recycled, it takes only five per cent of the energy and causes only five per cent of the pollution it would have taken for a can to be made from scratch.

"Tin" (steel) cans are what our vegetables, fruits and pet foods come packed in. Very little recycling has caught on with these so far, because the manufacturers of tin cans have not reaped great financial benefits from recycling them (even though recycling steel requires only 25 per cent of the energy used in making steel cans from virgin resources). The idea is catching on now because *consumers* are taking leadership in asking that cans be recycled. The EarthWorks Group says that Americans use enough steel cans to make a pipe that runs all the way from Los Angeles to New York and back again—*each day*. There is good reason for consumers to force the issue.

Other metals that make it into our lives are brass, copper, steel in other forms (your old car) and stainless steel (your old kitchen sink). All of them can be recycled.

To begin recycling these items, first contact your city dump to see whether its personnel sort for recycling. Your local recycling center and scrap-metal dealer would also be good contacts. Find out how they want the different metals sorted, and then set up recycling bins at home accordingly.

And as we suggested for paper and plastic, take a look around your office. Be an environmental activist there: volunteer your services to gather, sort and haul away the goods. You will probably need some help, because offices sometimes discard recyclable metals in heavier forms such as old desks (remember the army-issue style?), cabinets and file drawers. For large hauls, your local recycle center may be happy to do the carting.

As is typical with other recycling, money can be gotten for these goods, and your home or office can end up with a little extra cash or can support a worthwhile environmental cause.

6
Get Some Glass!

• • • • • • • • • • • •

If you have set up your system to process cans and plastics, then you are well on your way to taking care of your glass. The most interesting fact about glass is that it never really "dies." You can keep recycling it over and over. It's conceivable that, properly recycled, your glass will outlast you!

Here are some more interesting glass facts:

☐ Every two weeks Americans throw away enough glass containers to fill the 1,350-foot towers of the World Trade Center.

☐ Every ton of recycled glass saves a ton of resources it would have required to make that ton of glass from scratch.

☐ It takes about 65 per cent more energy to make a new ton of glass than to recycle a ton of glass.

Before you toss a wide-mouth mayonnaise jar, consider storing food or drink (leftover chili or salad, iced tea) in it in the fridge. It takes less space than a flat container—and what you see is what you've got.

If you're on the road and you buy a personal-size bottle of grapefruit juice at the 7-11, don't toss the empty bottle at the next stop. Take it home and wash it out. Fill several with a favorite juice and keep them chilled in the fridge, for easy grabbing and low cost.

Certain glass items cannot be recycled with your regular glass containers. These include mirrors, coffee pots, drinking glasses and baking dishes. If you need to get rid of such items, contact your local recycling center for advice.

As for your regular glass items, rinse them out, remove the metal lids and sort them according to colors—clear, brown and green (glass factories typically have to fill orders for specific colors). If you have a bunch of odd colors, ask your recycling-center staff what to do with them.

And again, we recommend that you carry the idea over into your workplace. Remember, every time you lug a five-pound bag of jars and bottles to the recycler, you've saved a supply of precious resources. And you've reduced planet clutter by a bagful.

7
Catch the Contaminants
· · · · · · · · · · · ·

We probably are not aware of the numbers and amounts of toxins that sit in our houses and offices and pass through our hands during normal everyday routines. Most of these can be recycled in some form but have to be treated with special care, separate from all other recyclable items. Here's a partial list:

☐ car batteries
☐ paint
☐ paint thinner
☐ charcoal lighter fluid
☐ nail polish
☐ nail polish remover
☐ oven and toilet cleaners

☐ sink and tub drain clog-busters
☐ garden pesticides
☐ antifreeze
☐ carpet cleaners
☐ caulking compound

First of all, contact your local recycling center to see what they will take. If they don't handle these toxins, your city government will have a federally mandated way to dispose of toxins.

The key elements in home recycling are (1) use up everything you can, (2) find a safe place, away from children, where the rest can be stored prior to being hauled away and (3) ensure a short storage life—that is, get them to the recycling center as soon as possible.

Some of these toxins—paint thinner, for example—can be turned into an alternative energy source by your recycling center. You can recycle paint at home by combining leftover paints and using the new combo on a painting project that does not require a specific color. Drop off your car battery at a local gas station—most states require car repair companies to recycle batteries, so they already have a system set up for disposal. A few waste-conscious retailers such as K-Mart will even pay you a dollar for your old car battery and then see that it gets to a recycler.

Another obvious step is: Don't buy more of these substances than you really need. When you can find a nontoxic alternative, use that instead.

8
Stamp Out Styrofoam

· · · · · · · · · · · ·

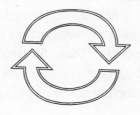

Perhaps you have seen the Burger King advertisement of a pyramid made from McDonald's styrofoam burger containers. That ad campaign was a brilliant, environmentally friendly nudge that influenced public opinion on McDonald's reluctance to switch to paper from styrofoam. As far as we know, styrofoam will *never* decompose—thus the effective "ancient pyramid" image—and one little styrofoam cup or box will potentially damage a spot of the ozone layer the size of a football field! We're talking dangerous stuff.

Almost no one recycles styrofoam at this point. The process consists of repackaging it into plastic-type products, mixing the styrofoam with other recycled plastics. The jury is still out on the future of styrofoam. It is conceivable that a decade from now styrofoam will exist basically as an encyclopedia entry and in landfills from days gone by.

We suggest simply cutting out the use of styrofoam in your home and office life. Whatever styrofoam you do collect should be recycled if at all possible. Wash out those McDonald's cups you couldn't avoid acquiring, and use them at your next few picnics till they start to leak. Use the tray from under the chicken parts you bought—it can be a saucer under a potted plant or a snack tray for Kool-Aid and cookies.

Try contacting the local university. They might be able to use your styrofoam for experimentation. As usual, contact your local government or recycling center, and contact the organizations listed in the resource section at the end of this book.

9
Get a Charge
· · · · · · · · · · · ·

We would like to suggest a simple, achievable envi-ronmental coup: Eliminate this nation's use of nonrechargeable batteries. All batteries require mercury for construction. In fact, 50 per cent of all mercury used in the United States goes to the manufacture of batteries.

So what's the big deal? Mercury is extremely toxic. It contaminates landfills and eventually makes its way into the atmosphere and water system.

Take a look around the house to see how many batteries are needed to run your life. Here is a partial checklist for American homes:

☐ flashlights
☐ clocks

☐ radios
☐ smoke alarms
☐ remote controls (TV, video, stereo, garage door)
☐ electronic games, baby dolls and toy animals
☐ Dad's gizmos
☐ electronic dictionary

You might wonder whether battery companies own America's toy industries: 40 per cent of this nation's battery sales are made during the Christmas season.

Our suggestion is simple. Go buy a recharging unit that accommodates a wide variety of batteries. You will probably pay $20 to $30 for a good one—less than next Christmas's battery bill. Set up the recharger in a convenient location and then take inventory of your battery-operated items. The next time those batteries fail you, go to Radio Shack and buy rechargeable batteries. Decide never to buy standard, disposable batteries again.

The next generation of children could laugh about disposable batteries in the same way that we laugh about the disposable clothes made in the mid-sixties. It can be done.

10
Hand-Me-Downs

· · · · · · · · · · · ·

At some point in our youth most of us feared being struck by the hand-me-down plague. Mom or Dad would pass on to us an older sibling's or relative's clothes. Being stuck with unfashionable clothes was probably what we hated most about this turn of events. Too bad Cousin Elmore didn't outgrow that suit while it was still in style!

We probably are not aware of the number of things we discard that could be of good use to someone else. We may replace items not because they are worn out but because we have grown tired of them or have been given a new one as a gift.

Rather than throwing away such items, give them to an organization that can ensure another life for them. Here is a sample list:

☐ clothes/shoes
☐ radios/clocks
☐ chairs/desks/beds/cabinets/tables
☐ garden tools
☐ television sets/lamps/vacuum cleaners/flashlights
☐ toys/games/baby equipment
☐ rugs/carpeting (including remnants)
☐ kitchen appliances (popcorn popper, blender, toaster, stove, can opener, refrigerator, hot plate)
☐ dishes/pots and pans/silverware/cooking utensils

We do not advocate giving junk to other people. That is always demeaning and inappropriate. We do suggest that anything of meaningful value and use not be discarded but recycled.

Go through your house, basement, tool shed and garage. Make a list of all reusable items, and then ask the folks at the neighborhood thrift store or Salvation Army outlet if they would like to pick them up. You'll be amazed to discover how much you've abandoned that is in perfectly good shape. Many of us don't want to throw away items that we have replaced, so they just gather dust rather than finding a new home.

One practical rule of thumb in recycling these sorts of materials is, "For every entry there is an exit." If you get a new sweater or pair of shoes, you must let go of one. Ditto for clocks, chairs, toys and all the rest. This is not always practical—for example, when you are setting up your household for the first time—but as a habit it will prevent the unnecessary stockpiling and waste of items that are useful to others.

11

Gray the Garden

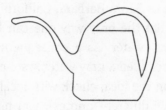

More than half of the water an average American family uses each day could be used again right at home, assuming the family has a yard.

We have a suggestion that is practical only for those who want to take a large step toward recycling. It costs some extra time and money but can make a wonderful difference in recycling the precious resource of water.

You can replumb your home to redirect all of your water, except what is used in the toilet, for use in the garden. If you have the cash reserves, the cost of doing this will be recouped from your water bill over a period of three to five years. If you are currently building a home, you can plumb the house ahead of time and have virtually no additional expense. Once you have replumbed your home (which includes a storage tank for the captured water), begin to use soaps and detergents that are friendly to lawns and gardens. Most large stores carry these items. If you are unable to locate them, check our resources at the back of this book.

The water that you have saved is called "gray water." We predict that several cities will soon enact construction codes that require plumbing new homes and apartments for gray water. In cities such as Santa Barbara, California, the water shortage is so severe that the only way one can legally water one's garden is with gray water. As a consequence, many residents have voluntarily installed a gray water system.

To get started on the idea, check with local plumbers (be sure to get two or three different quotes); you might check as well with local government. Your city may be progressive enough to provide a consulting service to help residents "go gray."

12
Precycle

• • • • • • • • • • • •

How about approaching the recycle campaign at the "front end" of the problem? As much as one-third of all paper waste is from packaging. We could cut back the amount of recycling we do at home and reduce the amount of natural resources used up in recycling (energy at the recycling plant) if we shopped with "precycling" in mind.

Here are a few suggestions:

☐ Don't buy individual cans of pop. Buy the large containers and use glasses at home.

☐ Do the same with milk and other beverages—always go for the larger container.

☐ Don't wrap your vegetables at the fresh produce section.

They will make it home just fine without a plastic bag.

☐ Buy long-life items in bulk when possible—for example, flour, sugar, rice, beans. Store them in containers at home.

☐ Be careful when buying snacks. Too often each candy is individually wrapped and chips are divided unnecessarily among small packets. Buy the big package and make your own personal-size ones if needed, using reusable baggies.

☐ Be conscious of the number of bags you acquire at the mall—bookstore, music store, electronics store, clothes shop, jewelry shop. One or two bags would probably handle all these items. Just add new purchases to the bag you were given at the previous stop. Or carry a canvas or nylon tote.

☐ Avoid items that won't easily recycle—for example, styrofoam egg cartons.

Here are some interesting statistics that can motivate us toward precycling:

☐ One dollar out of every ten we spend on food goes to packaging.

☐ An average American throws away a total of 60 pounds of plastic each year.

☐ A fast-food burger bag has an actual use-life of less than 30 seconds.

☐ The long cardboard box encasing your to-be-purchased CD has *no use*.

13
Reduced Use Zone Ahead
• • • • • • • • • • • •

Your precycling habits can extend beyond shopping.
Consider turning your home into a Reduced Garbage Zone.
When less waste goes out the door, fewer trees and other resources get spent in replacing it. Try some of these ideas:

☐ Save paper you get from committee meetings, school or the office which is photocopied on one side. Use the other side for note pads or writing rough drafts for school.

☐ Do the same with computer printouts. The age of computers allows us to print out roughs for correcting. Term papers, financial statements and proposals add tons to our cities' landfills every year.

☐ Whenever practical, use both sides of your legal note pad, reporter's pad or binder paper.

☐ Say good-by to paper plates and cups in home use. They are fine for picnics.

☐ You might go a step further and eliminate paper napkins. No-iron cloth napkins are simple to care for and add a touch of elegance to your table. Make a distinctive napkin ring for each family member and extras for guests.

☐ Go easy on the paper towels. Most spills on counters and tabletops can be cleaned with the dishcloth.

☐ If you're an avid coffee drinker, purchase a metal coffee filter that replaces the disposable paper filters.

Be sure to apply these ideas at the office as well. Overcome the sense that you're being "too picky" or stingy. You're being visionary and caring. Large corporations are catching on to the value of reducing garbage. As recently as April 1991, McDonald's announced its intention to reduce its garbage by 80 per cent! You're on the winning team.

14
Adopt-a-
Block
· · · · · · · · · · · ·

Once you have learned the art of recycling in your home, we recommend that you spread the good news. Our guess is that most people don't recycle simply because they are not familiar with how easy the process is. Why not transform your block, apartment building or school dorm into a recycle zone?

Setting up the process would take a couple of solid weekends, after which maintaining the process could take as little as an hour a week. Begin with a little research: How is recycling currently being practiced on your block? Does the city get involved? Are there typical recyclable items that are heavily used in your area?

Once you have all the information, take action. If you live in a dorm or apartment building, be sure to work with the resident directors or managers. You will need to establish a central drop-off point at your building or on your block. This will include containers for items such as newspapers, plastics, tin/steel, glass, oil and cardboard. If it's on your block, you might donate a small portion of your yard to the cause.

If a good number of people join in, you will require help in transporting the material for recycling. Perhaps you can get support from a neighbor, or, if there is enough material to make it financially worthwhile, the recycling center may do the honors.

When the system is in place, get the word out. We recommend both a community meeting where people are invited to hear about the idea and a door-to-door campaign where you explain the notion and distribute literature clarifying the dropoff system. The idea will gain momentum as neighbors watch others catch on.

You may well find that the money gained from the recycling more than covers the cost of running the program. You may even consider giving a surprise Christmas bonus back to the neighbors with any leftover funds at the end of the year.

Once you are happy with how the idea is working, inform the university or city hall of its success. Your recycling efforts may get multiplied as others hear about them and pick up the idea.

15
Adopt-an-
Office
· · · · · · · · · · · ·

If you have managed to bring recycling into your com-
pany, how about a bigger and braver step? Adopt the entire office
building or, if not too large, the entire office block. You will
need a motivated team of assistants, but once the system is in
place it will run pretty well with little maintenance.

Here is how we suggest you proceed: Let your boss in on the
idea. Tell him or her that you want to carry recycling to other
local businesses, using yours as a model of how it can work.
Once you have your boss's blessing, do the research. Find out
how many other businesses there are on the block (or in the
building), list their services, find out their current recycling
practices and jot down the items they most frequently discard.

From this list you will be able to determine what kind of recycling center you will need to establish on location. Be sure to get all of that in place, including the transport system, before going to the other companies. It's best to ensure that there are no hitches in the process, because people do not need any discouragement.

Make up a simple package containing four sheets of paper. Page 1 should be a very short note on company letterhead, signed by your boss, expressing his or her support for the idea since it has worked so well for the company. Page 2 would be "10 Easy Ways to Recycle," preferably done on a desktop design program (Kinko's will help you for a small fee). Page 3 would explain the location for dropping off the to-be-recycled material, and page 4 would give the names and phone numbers of persons to contact if there are any questions or problems in the process.

Take this package and go business-to-business. Inquire who the best person is to implement the idea, secure an appointment and then sign up another environmentally conscious company!

From time to time, go back to these same persons to see how the system is working for them and to suggest some additional ways to increase recycling. Once the system is well in place and operating with class, we suggest that you report the program to city hall as a model program for the entire town or city.

16
Adopt-a-Road
. . . .

You may already have seen the signs along highways in some states: "This portion of the highway adopted by the Boy Scouts of _____ ." The idea of taking responsibility for a portion of road is a great way to recycle and keep the environment beautiful.

For some reason, junk collects. Perhaps it is one of those laws of the universe: *Any void will eventually be filled with available garbage.* We suggest a vigorous defeat of that law.

The garbage that collects along highways may end up in streams, polluting our water source, harming vegetation and killing insects and fish. Or that same trash may blow across the street, be picked up by a conscientious neighbor and be thrown into the bin, where it is ready to head off to the landfill.

By adopting a stretch of highway, you interrupt this process. Proceeding with the idea is fairly simple. Scout out a piece of road. Pick a stretch that is particularly nasty. Collect a trash can full of discards and then make a trip to city hall. Explain where you picked up the garbage and outline your plan to organize a group to adopt that mile or two. Most city halls would be delighted to cooperate. Find out if there are any regulations you will need to observe, ask them to provide the trash bags and reflective vests for the workers, arrange a dropoff location for the recyclable goods and ask the city to set up signs on that stretch of road announcing that it has been adopted by your group.

Find your volunteers. Your first clean-up will probably take an entire Saturday. Divide your team into types of trash—for example, paper, plastics, glass, tin and "other." Arm them with the appropriate bags and then systematically comb your stretch of highway. Once you have collected all the trash and piled it into one pickup truck, take a photo for future PR purposes and then go to a pizza restaurant to celebrate. Divide the team into weekly subteams so that everyone has a two-hour duty once a month. This way some small group is out there every week making sure the trash level is kept low.

When the project is working well, contact your local newspaper. Explain what you have done, provide your PR photograph and see if it will run a special-interest story on your efforts. You may find that other groups will join the campaign.

17
Convert Your Church
● ● ● ● ● ● ● ● ● ● ● ● ●

Every Sunday, approximately 22 million Americans drive to church. The recycling potential of this God-loving, creation-caring group of people is just mind-boggling! Each Sunday of the year has the potential of becoming an environmental act of worshiping God. Unfortunately, and all too often accurately, the church has been accused of being insensitive to the concerns of the green movement. Well, let's trash that notion.

Consider taking on the task of converting your church to recycling consciousness. It's the perfect setup: You have property, you have a newsletter (the bulletin), you have a transport system (members all drive there weekly) and you have a good reason—you all love God the Creator. Talk with your pastor. He or she may be willing to dedicate one entire Sunday to the issue, for starters. The pastor's role will be to preach a sermon on caring for the garden, and your role will be to explain how the system is going to work.

Again, you need to have the system in place ahead of time. Set up all the recycling bins at a convenient location on the church property (convenient in this case means easy access for a truck to haul the stuff off). Clearly label the different containers. Design a simple, attractive insert for the church bulletin describing how the system works. Members can bring newspapers, plastic, aluminum, tin, whatever you are able to pass along to a recycling center.

Every Sunday, have a few teenagers serve in the "green brigade." Their function is to collect bags from cars as they drive into the church parking lot. This increases convenience to church members, gets teens involved, and creates more visibility for the practice (enhancing the likelihood that people will stick with the idea).

Now the fun part. The most underfunded program in the churches of America is missionary outreach. Our suggestion is that *all* the proceeds from recycling go to a special mission fund beyond the regular mission giving. This fund could be turned into a special Christmas check that goes to each of the church's missionaries for personal use (something they always need). What a satisfying way of celebrating the whole gospel of Jesus Christ—that is, caring for souls *and* caring for creation.

18
Clean Sweep
· · · · · · · · · · · ·

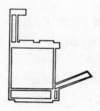

Over time, major garbage items collect in our back yards, basements, garages, alleyways and sheds. Some of the garbage may be toxic, but typically it is "stuff" that we figured we'd eventually get to. The problem is that one day, in a burst of energy, we do get to those piles. And typically what happens is that we load it all in a U-Haul or Acme rental and cart it off to the dump. We feel much better for having cleaned up the eyesore, but in fact we have just contributed to an environmental problem by stuffing the landfill unnecessarily.

Our suggestion is to take advantage of the human desire for a clean sweep and *organize* a coordinated effort ahead of an impulse-driven blitz. This is what you can do: Get a clipboard and take a walk around the block. Tell the neighbors that you are arranging a "yard day" when a truck will be coming door to door to collect any large items that cannot be set out on trash day. Find out what sorts of materials they want to get rid of—couches, stoves, tires, branches, paint, whatever. Get a general idea of what size task you're taking on. Once you're pretty sure you have a grasp of what's ahead, approach the people at city hall or your local recycling center and tell them that you are able to arrange the labor for a clean sweep of your block if they will provide the trucks.

When the system is in place, go back to your neighbors with a flyer announcing the pickup day. Tell them what time to have their material ready at curbside and how it needs to be sorted. Organize a crew of volunteer laborers and assign them to specific types of recyclable items. Put the hefty volunteers with the truck that will cart away scrap iron, stoves, desks and the like, and assign the petite laborers to lighter items.

Part of your plan is to deliver each item to its most appropriate destination: the Salvation Army or Goodwill, a resale shop that uses its proceeds to stock a food pantry, a recycling center or, when necessary, the town dump. Check with all of them in advance regarding what they'll accept (and whether the dump charges a fee).

If you are able to execute this operation fairly easily, your neighborhood and city hall will welcome a repeat every six months. You may even find the whole city catching on.

19
Elderly
Aid
· · · · · · · · · · · ·

How about combining your recycling efforts with assis-tance to the elderly?

First of all, find out where the elderly are. You may discover that in your town the majority of them live in convalescent centers. If so, offer your time and organizational skills to the center in the same way you would for your dorm, office building or apartment complex. Very often those who are working for the elderly are exhausted from the demands that go with that kind of work, and so they cannot easily picture themselves taking on an additional concern. Your willingness to take charge of recycling will be greatly appreciated by them.

You or your group may be aware of where many elderly people

live who do not receive the care of a larger organization. Perhaps you know several elderly people through your church or fellowship group. Decide how many you are willing to help and find the best way to approach these senior citizens. It's important that you not go to them outside of an established relationship, because, sadly, many of the elderly have been victims of unscrupulous salespersons and consequently they are not very open to strangers.

Make the task as simple as possible. Most elderly people (with some dramatic exceptions) are not likely to generate as much trash as other people, so provide one sturdy plastic trash can for *all* their recyclable goods and a list of what they can put in it. Drive by twice a month to collect the goods (simply sort the material into your truck on location), and return the trash can to them before moving on to the next home. Use gloves to protect yourself from germs and cuts during the sorting process.

A fringe benefit here will be your regular contact with some lonely people who will appreciate your brief visits and your cheerful words. And you'll be helping direct some "trash" away from cluttering the planet and toward new usefulness.

20
Start Your Own Company

· · · · · · · · · · · ·

Okay, here's the project for the real visionaries who have the time and business skills. Perhaps you live in a town where there is inadequate recycling help. This is your chance to stand in the gap!

Begin with careful research. We recommend that you first contact your state office, city hall and national resource center (listed in the resource section at the end of this book) to find out all the laws (both federal and state), pitfalls and recommendations that go with a recycling business. Once you are sure you're getting to understand the basics, travel to at least three other towns where a recycling center is in operation. Talk with the owners. Nothing beats advice that comes from a practitioner.

Your next step is to locate property. There is a good chance that city hall or a local business will be willing to get you started with donated facilities. Both government and business people feel the need for recycling. When your building is lined up and you have a sense of how much volume you are going to process, contact the recycling corporations you've located that want to buy your product. Have them provide the shipping container and replace it every time they collect a full container.

With your system in place, get the word out. You may consider beginning with limited hours—say, all day Saturday—and then adding hours as business demands. Publicize your services in the local newspaper, and be sure to give very clear instructions regarding what types of items you can process. Publish your payment rates too.

If the business takes off, you may consider taking leadership in coordinating weekly curbside pickups, highway clean-sweeps, business carting and even city government recycling (in cooperation with your local landfill corporation).

II

Water

• • • • • • • • • • • • • •

By far the single largest death-inducing factor in the world today is contaminated water. Perhaps as many as 30 million people die from it *per year* and, sadly, as many as two-thirds of them are children under the age of five. To be concerned about clean, safe water is an environmental commitment that is very distinctly pro-life.

Water, water, everywhere,
And all the boards did shrink;
Water, water, everywhere,
Nor any drop to drink.
—Samuel Taylor Coleridge, *The Rime of the Ancient Mariner*

When the poet wrote of sailors adrift on the ocean, dying of thirst even though they were surrounded by water, little did he know how accurate a picture he was drawing of a modern society nearly two centuries later.

Water is contaminated through improper trash disposal, toxic waste, air pollution (brought down by the rain), runoff from pesticides and fertilizers, underground fuel storage tanks and sewage.

And water is scarce. Only one per cent of the world's total water supply is potable. Fresh water supply may one day be the world's chief weapon. The 1991 Persian Gulf war demonstrated human vulnerability in regard to water when a major desalinization plant supplying clean water to Saudi Arabia was threatened by an oil slick, and when thousands of Kurdish refugees fleeing Iraq died each day due to a lack of water in their makeshift camps.

Water is the Achilles heel of Los Angeles, where citizens are fined for hosing down their sidewalks or consuming more than 350 gallons per day per household. The San Joaquin Valley, the world's fresh fruit and vegetable capital, had its water source cut by 80 per cent during 1991. Israel, while pursuing a program of rapid expansion in Gaza and the West Bank, shipping in hundreds of thousands of Soviet Jews, faces the prospect of virtually no drinking water in the country by the year 2000.

We suggest five simple ways you can make a difference to planet earth's future as far as water takes us there.

21
Check the Flow
....

We waste water every day without even trying and without even knowing it. Millions of gallons seep into America's sewer without our help. So the point is, we've got to take action and check that flow.

Check Your Faucets
It may appear to be just a trickle, but the little drops add up to an enormous loss of fresh water. Make it a Saturday project to inspect every faucet in the house and outside. If you find any leaks, get into action. Let's hope that the solution is as simple as replacing a washer. If you know how to do these simple plumbing jobs, go for it. Otherwise, seek the help of a friend.

If you rent a house or apartment, leaky faucets are the concern of the landlord. Contact him or her immediately.

Check Your Toilet

There are two ways in which your toilet may be a silent culprit. The first is a faulty valve that lets water into the bowl when you flush. To see if you have that problem, get a colored water freshener for toilets (from your supermarket) and put it in the toilet water tank. Leave your toilet undisturbed for ten minutes; then check to see if the water in the bowl has changed color. If so, change the valve.

Another culpable deed your toilet may be performing is sending too much water through on every flush. You can typically cut that back by as much as a third and still get all the flushing you need. We recommend that you take a gallon glass jar, fill it with water and set it inside your tank away from the flushing mechanism. Voilà! You've saved a gallon per flush. Most hardware or plumbing stores carry a kit for reducing water storage in toilet tanks. See what your local store offers if the glass jar doesn't work.

Check the Shower

Although a typical shower uses less water than a typical bath, much more water flows out of the spout than is necessary for a good shower. If you have not already done so, install a little washer that restricts the flow of water through the shower head. Again, most hardware stores can help you find the part you need, and if you live in a water-conscious city, the local government may provide the part gratis.

22
Reduce the Flow: Indoors
· · · · · · · · · · ·

Nothing conserves water like saving water. Our sug-gestion, then, is very simple: Consciously cut back on the amount of water you allow to flow through the faucets of your home and workplace every day.

When you do the dishes, don't leave the faucet running the whole time in order to rinse as you go. Fill the other side of the sink (or a second dishpan) for rinsing. Then the tub of used rinse water will do double duty if you put it on plants and bushes rather than down the drain. Or, if you prefer to rinse under running water, stack the dishes in the rinsing area, then turn on the faucet long enough to quickly rinse them all. A low-volume aerator spray faucet will enable you to do this easily and with much less water.

Think through your other uses of water in the same way.

The Global Tomorrow Coalition has created a helpful comparison chart on how to save water. We have reproduced part of it to help make our point and encourage your conservation:

	Saving Water	**Wasting Water**
Shower	Wet down, soap up rinse off (4 gallons)	Regular shower (25 gallons)
Tub Bath	May we suggest a shower?	Full tub (36 gallons)
Toilet	Install a jar or kit, minimize flushing to save a gallon per flush.	Normal flush uses 5-7 gallons.
Washing Hands	Full basin (1 gallon)	Running water (2 gallons)
Shaving	Full basin (1 gallon)	Tap running (20 gallons)
Brushing Teeth	Wet brush, rinse briefly (1/2 gallon)	Tap running (10 gallons)
Leaks	Report immediately.	A small drip wastes 25 gallons per day.

23
Reduce the Flow: Outdoors
· · · · · · · · · · · · ·

We have suggested how to reduce water flow inside your home. Now let's go outside. We assume that you've already checked your faucets for leakage. The issue now is to reduce the amount of water you use.

Caring for the Garden

If you keep a lawn or grow vegetables or flowers, you need to water them. But you can take care to conserve water in the garden in three ways. The first idea we mentioned earlier: *gray water*. This is by far the most effective means to reduce water consumption, because it allows you to put back to work what was headed down the drain. Your second option is to carefully choose the *time of day* you water. Early morning and evening are best. If the sun is up and strong, you will lose a good amount of water to evaporation. Consequently, you will water longer to keep the garden green. Third, watch closely for any unnecessary *runoff.* Often a small stream of water ends up going down the curb into a storm drain. If you cannot operate the sprinkler in certain areas without a runoff, we suggest that you water those spots by hand.

Cleaning the Car

We have two suggestions for conserving water while cleaning the car. The first is to *use a bucket* for as much of the process as possible, rather than a running hose. The impact is comparable to washing your hands in a sinkful of water versus under a running flow. Second, wash your car *on the lawn*—achieve two purposes at the same time. Buy a detergent for your car that is friendly to lawns, or dispense with soaps and use plain water.

Cleaning the Walk

Don't use a hose to clean your driveway or sidewalk. All those gallons of water are wasted gallons. Rather, pull out the push broom and give your body a workout. And if you notice an elderly neighbor trying to do the same, offer your youthful frame in environmental service!

24
Keep It Clean

. . . .

At the beginning of this section we explained how pol-
luted water kills. And the fact that only one per cent of the
world's water is potable suggests that we ought to keep clean
whatever little bit of water we have. We have two recommendations for keeping it clean.

Adopt-a-Stream
Here is your chance to lead a group effort to make America
beautiful. Scout out the streams in your area and decide which
one appears to be most polluted. Ask city hall if your group
could have the responsibility to keep it clean.

Organize a workday to give the stream a thorough sweep, and

as much as possible, sort through the retrieved trash for recyclable objects. Take advantage of the PR potential of this task and get a photo of your group in action in case your local newspaper considers your efforts newsworthy (you may influence others to get into the act). Divide your volunteer group into subgroups so that every week someone is doing a fresh sweep of the stream. If the city allows it, have a sign erected on location that identifies this as an adopted stream.

If you would like to pursue this idea a little further, how about securing the help of biologists at your local university to find out about the natural vegetation and animal/insect life that go with that stream? Learn how your cleanup efforts encourage the natural growth of God's handiwork.

Control the Pollutants
Our second recommendation is that you take care not to pour any toxins down the drain and ensure that you are recycling them (rather than allowing them to be carted off to the landfill, where they're sure to eventually make it back into the water system). Also, reduce your purchases of these items, and that will diminish the chance of inadvertently polluting water with them.

25
Make a Career of It
· · · · · · · · · · · ·

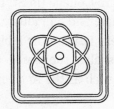

Everyone can make a difference in keeping the flow of our precious water tight and in keeping it pure. Some may want to make a lifetime vocation out of it.

The opportunities in the field are endless. You could consider any of the following, for example:

☐ well digging
☐ sanitation-plant management
☐ community development
☐ education
☐ engineering
☐ dam construction (where environmentally sound)
☐ public health

Education for these and many other careers related to caring for water can be obtained at most large state universities. If you are interested in working internationally in this field, universities such as UCLA are well equipped to bring Third World sensitivities to the subject.

If you are interested in receiving a Christian education as part of your preparation, Wheaton College (in Wheaton, Illinois) has a good undergraduate program called HNGR (Human Needs and Global Resources). Eastern College (in St. Davids, Pennsylvania) has both an undergraduate and a graduate program that look at international development issues from a biblical orientation. Its biology department has also sponsored environmental study tours of crucial regions such as the Amazon Basin.

III

Energy

• • • • • • • • • • • • • • • •

Environmentalists predicted it for years, and finally it happened—the world entered a major war over energy.

The Persian Gulf crisis will be with the world for many years to come. Fear that Saddam Hussein's invasion of Kuwait would lead to a shortage in the world oil supply resulted in a U.S.-led military response that has crippled the economies of both Kuwait and Iraq, created the earth's most disastrous environmental nightmare with the pollution of seven hundred ignited oil wells, left hundreds of thousands of civilians dead and spurred three million civilians to become political refugees. We are more vulnerable to our energy needs than we know.

The United States consumes more than 25 per cent of the world's energy. We are only five per cent of the world's population. We cannot justify our energy consumption based on our production of goods and services. The U. S., according to *Time* magazine, has less than half the economic output of either Germany or Japan. Simply put, we are a consumer nation, and our inordinate share of the energy pie might be considered immoral.

The world is unstable because of our dependence on energy resources (exemplified by the Gulf war). The world's energy reserves are threatened by our overindulgent lifestyle. And our use of energy from fossil fuels (such as oil) is constantly polluting the environment and hence, according to the Global Tomorrow Coalition, "harming human health, causing acid rain damage to entire ecosystems, and increasing the buildup of atmospheric carbon dioxide and the likelihood of global warming and climate instability" *(The Global Energy Handbook,* p. 192).

We're concerned. Here are five simple steps many of us could take to conserve energy.

26
Go
Natural
· · · · · · · · · · · ·

Well, almost. There are ways to keep yourself warm or cool, whichever the need might be, without consuming too much energy.

Keeping Cool
The air conditioner is not the only resource you have for staying cool. If your house is well insulated, we suggest that you keep your home cooled down in the following ways.

Watch the pattern of the sun around your house. Which side gets hottest? At what time of day is that part of the house still pleasant? While the outside is pleasantly cool, keep your windows open. During the hottest part of the summer that will be late evening through early morning. Just before the air begins to warm up on you, close all the windows. You have trapped the cool air inside.

Now, close all the blinds and curtains on the sun side of the house. This will prevent the rays from baking your cooled rooms. If you have a large picture window on the sun side, you might consider a special thermal curtain that keeps out most of that heat. (Inquire at a hardware or department store.) If practical, close the doors to the rooms on that side of the house to create an additional air-insulation lock against the heat. A couple of good ceiling fans in the remainder of the house could potentially render your air conditioner silent for the duration of the summer.

Consider the option of planting a large shade tree or two on the sun side of the house. Choose one that will lose its leaves in the winter, so that you can benefit from the sun during cold weather.

Keeping Warm
First of all, experiment with your thermostat. You may have more heat pouring through the system than is really necessary. A well-insulated house does not need to be heated above 68 degrees Fahrenheit. If your house is not well insulated, pushing the thermostat higher only warms the snow outside. You may find that you are comfortable with the thermostat set as low as 63 degrees.

If your home is empty during the day, make sure the thermostat is lowered. At night, don't warm all the house with the furnace; take advantage of heavy PJs, flannel sheets and lots of blankets as much as possible to keep warm. Again, try this with the thermostat set low.

Think of certain areas of the house as your "living quarters" during the winter's worst. Close the doors and heating vents to the rest of the house, and keep your energy drain confined to that smaller area. This, too, will help to insulate your home further from the outside (closed-off rooms provide an air lock). If you are able to, include the kitchen in your living quarters. The heat generated by your stove, oven and refrigerator will help keep the temperature up. If you have ceiling fans, keep them going—they will push the warm air down to your level.

27
Patch the Leaks
· · · · · · · · · · · ·

Here is a depressing fact: All the oil that is shipped via the Alaska Pipeline for use in the United States is lost to the atmosphere through leaks in America's homes. Of course it is not the exact same oil, but it is an equivalent amount.

We can do something about that.

Once again, contact your local utility company. If you live in an older home, let the company know that you want a check done on your home for energy leaks. Most will gladly perform the check. The most typical areas of energy loss will be through doors, windows and attic. Fixing these leaks can cost less than the amount you will save on your utility bills over one year. The utility company will provide you with a simple guide to fixing the leaks (if not, your hardware store, library or local government will help). Typically it will involve laying down insulation in the attic and weatherstripping your windows and doors. The whole process may take a couple of days.

If you live in an extreme climate, there are some additional considerations. First, you may need climate-proof window panes. If so, the cost may take several years to recoup through your utility bill (unless the leakage is very severe), but the long-term savings will be great, and the world's energy supply will last longer. You may also need to insulate your walls and floor. Certain states in regions where winters are long and severe will do that work for you—materials and labor free of charge. Contact your city hall to see whether your house qualifies for this help.

Fortunately, progressive building codes are beginning to require that these energy-savers are in place from the outset. Eventually all old buildings will be required to conform to new standards or be destroyed.

28
Step in Line
·············

Every day America's cars belch four billion pounds of carbon dioxide into the air. It may be American to express our individualism and independence through our motor vehicles, but it is also lethal. More than that, it makes us *dependent* (contrary to our self-perception) in that we require the resources and cooperation of other nations. The Gulf war illustrates that all too clearly.

Forward-looking former president Jimmy Carter proposed legislation and lifestyle changes that would have completely eliminated our need for foreign oil had we implemented them when they were suggested—during the seventies. Those ideas of his are suddenly becoming very attractive to lawmakers and private citizens in the nineties.

We propose a few very simple lifestyle changes that could

make a big difference in the environment and the availability of resources.

Feet First

First, walk or ride a bike whenever possible. Every step you take with your own feet is a positive and important contribution to a better world. And it is probably good for your body too.

Go Public

Second, may we suggest public transport? Most large cities offer it, and once you begin to incorporate the system into your lifestyle you will wonder how you ever got along without it. Someone else fights the traffic, gets the heartburn and suffers frayed nerves. You read the paper or your favorite novel. (Chicago recently held a "Beat the Backup" Day, urging commuters to leave their cars at home. In a test, one suburban passenger boarded Amtrak and the other jumped in his car. The first to arrive at the destination point in the city was the one on the train—by far. Even if your city isn't taking action, *you* can.)

Go Together

Third, we suggest that you carpool whenever possible. If you work for a large firm, it will likely arrange carpooling for you at your request. Or take leadership. Certain tax laws reward carpooling with your own vehicle. Inquire into the specific code, and then look for people ready to go with you on this environmentally sound journey.

Finally, if you must drive alone, think through your errands and combine them so that you make as few solo trips as possible.

29
Go Lite on Lights

· · · · · · · · · · · ·

If you are not sure of the benefits of keeping your lights low, leave them all on around the clock for a full month and then take a good look at the electricity bill. The drain on energy resources and your pocketbook will be significant.

Although this idea is quite uncomplicated, we consider it very important. We have two suggestions in particular.

Turn Them Off
Just don't use the lights when you don't have to. "Any unoccupied room is an unlit room" is a simple enough guideline to follow. According to the World Resources Institute, 20 per cent of America's electricity is consumed by light bulbs.

Change the Bulbs

With a little extra cash you can convert certain lights to fluorescent bulbs. The bulbs cost considerably more but will last up to *ten years*. Fluorescent bulbs are most efficient when left on (that's right) for a couple of hours, so choose the rooms in your house where you are more likely to spend two or more hours at a time each day. Consult your friendly hardware person when you are ready to make the switch.

30
Watch Those Appliances
· · · · · · · · · · · · ·

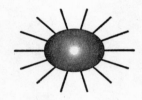

You may have some energy busters in your home. Some appliances are just plain nasty to the environment. They consume much more energy than they need to produce the intended effect.

Many cities throughout the U.S. are catching on to the fact that good appliances mean a more secure future. Most utility companies are quite willing to do a free inspection of your house and make recommendations regarding your wares—these include the fridge, freezer, water heater and heating and cooling system. If any of these appliances turn out to be disastrous energy consumers, you want to begin thinking about replacing them. Or there may be simple steps you can take to make them less inefficient.

Just Beginning?

Perhaps you are setting up home for the first time and are in a position to buy your major appliances. If so, this is a time for "precycling." Major appliances displayed in stores carry energy-usage information labels. Find out from *Consumer's Guide* which brands are reliable, and then get the comparison sheet out to pick the brand that both fits your budget and goes easy on the environment.

If you are in a position to put in a new heating and cooling system, be sure to get advice on what type of system will give you the comfort you need while being good to the air and easy on the energy supply. Contact the organizations listed in the resource section in this book, and consult your local government and your utility companies.

Try the Sun

If you are particularly good with your hands and have a little spare time and money, consider taking advantage of the sun. You can get all the hot water you need in the summer without the help of gas or electricity. Some state governments offer tax incentives if you convert part of your home to solar energy. Give them a call. Several very "user-friendly" manuals have been written for homeowners who want to go in this direction.

IV

Shop Green

. . . .

Our approach in this section on "shopping green" is really quite straightforward. If we're going to recycle goods, then let's buy those goods once they show up in a recycled form, and in our buying let's demonstrate a clear commitment to companies and products that are friendly to God's planet.

Consumers have much more power than they realize. Companies will change entire policies if they fear that the consumer will abandon them. Your careful shopping is a positive vote for a healthy planet, and through it you join forces with a very large number of other Americans who have begun to understand the force behind their pocketbooks.

Every trip you make to the store can be an act of environmental stewardship. We suggest five ways you can make a difference at the cash register.

31
Green
Gifts
. . . .

Is it true that most Americans have everything they really need? It seems that way at Christmas and on birthdays. Here is a great opportunity to buy green. Your gifts will probably be something your friends and relatives have never received before. And this kind of gift can educate them regarding our planet's need for friendly care. We suggest the following possibilities:

☐ Give a gift subscription to *Greenpeace* or *Garbage* magazine.

☐ Get the gift catalog from Greenpeace and order gift items.

☐ Look for games that teach about the environment.

☐ Purchase greeting cards that are clearly marked as recycled.

☐ Find an easy-to-read book (such as this one?) that will help the person take specific steps toward caring for the planet.

☐ Give a small tree or plant with gardening instructions.

☐ Give a gift pass to an exhibit or activity that encourages love for nature—for example, the zoo or a whale-watching cruise.

☐ Offer a picnic lunch in conjunction with a nature walk on a day of their choosing.

☐ Give a coupon that is good for two or three hours of your services to help set up a recycling center in their home.

☐ Finally, give a labor coupon that offers your services to spend half a day with them doing a clean sweep of their yard, garage and whatever else needs a little environmental attention.

32
Buy Local
· · · · · · · · · · · ·

The less distance your product has to travel to get to you, the less fuel burned, the less wear on tires, the less packaging (and hence waste) needed, the less climate control required (and hence less energy consumed) and the less likelihood that certain preservatives (toxins) are added to your food (and thus the water system eventually) to keep it looking good till it gets to your kitchen.

Is that a case for buying local?

We think so.

Check Out Your Store

Do a little research. Find out from your grocer where the store's products hail from. Let him or her know that you are interested in buying locally as much as possible, and ask for a tour of the produce, meat, cheese, milk and fruit sections. Get as specific as possible. If you live in a small town, you have a much better chance of getting cooperation. Offer your creativity to a willing grocer. Suggest the creation of a special green label that sports the message "Locally Grown." Put an ad in the local paper announcing this innovation, and ask the editors for their cooperation in explaining to the public the environmental value of supporting regional producers. Local growers will be behind you.

Encourage Farm Co-ops
If a little bit of real estate nearby is available good for raising vegetables and fruit, join with some others who understand the value of a unified effort to produce your own goods. The idea of a co-op is that everyone puts in a proportional amount of money and labor to reap a proportional reward. This may be a small plot in someone's back yard or an empty lot whose owner lets you use it. If you are business-oriented, you might even experiment with this idea as something that could grow into a large regional company.

Some cities have successfully set up a Saturday-morning "green market" for people who grow their own fruits and vegetables and want to sell them to the public. This is easy enough to coordinate if you are willing to put in the extra effort it would require, and once the idea catches on it is very hard to squelch. People who are used to getting everything canned and highly processed enjoy handling food a little closer to its original state. And the weekly sojourn becomes a time of socializing with new friends.

97

33
Look for the Labels
· · · · · · · · · · ·

You may be surprised by the degree to which environ-
mentally friendly products are making their way into grocery and
hardware stores. It may require an extra few minutes every time
you shop to check out the labels, but it is well worth your while
if you want to work for a better environment.

Basically, you are interested in knowing whether the product
was made from or packaged with exclusively virgin materials or
whether the manufacturer took the care to recycle. The label will
say something like "Made with 50% recycled paper" or "This
bottle is made partially with recycled glass." The types of items
you most want to check on are the following:

☐ napkins
☐ cartons, boxes
☐ glasses, jars, bottles
☐ tins, cans
☐ cards, envelopes, note pads
☐ plastic implements and tools
☐ plastic containers
☐ paints and thinners
☐ picnic wares
☐ clothes (for example, ski-jacket lining)
☐ tires
☐ carpeting

We've already suggested that you "precycle" at the store, and that involves both buying products that are not overpackaged (leading to more waste) and buying materials that you know are easily recycled or made from recycled material.

34
Buying Big
· · · · · · · · · · · ·

If the readership of this book looks anything like the national demographics, then one-third of you will be buying a house in the future. If you are among this number, you are entering an enormous realm of environmental consideration. Here are some of the typical environmental questions that go with owning a house:

☐ Is it insulated?

☐ Does the heating/cooling system reflect low energy usage? Will you have solar options?

☐ Are the major appliances low on energy consumption?

☐ Is the construction material from recycled goods where possible?

☐ Are the windows climate-proof?

☐ Does the construction take advantage of the sun's patterns?

Be sure to check with utility companies and find out about city coding regulations to see whether there are any other questions or considerations that are worth exploring. For a while it was fashionable for Americans to buy homes simply as investment properties. Moves were made quite regularly. That pattern is shifting as citizens are reflecting on the value of a quieter, more stable lifestyle. You are likely to fall into that statistical category, so think long-term. Which means think environmentally sound.

The other "big buy" you will likely consider is a vehicle. If possible, stay away from two types—diesel engines, because they spew unacceptable amounts of sulfur into the atmosphere, and leaded-gasoline vehicles (older used cars), because they put poisonous lead back into the atmosphere. And then look for vehicles that are low on gas mileage. Unfortunately, American-built cars are still lagging in the quest to reduce vehicles' demands for fuel.

Finally, if you are considering taking leadership in carpooling, inquire with your company and friends and coworkers to see how likely that option is, and then investigate the possibility of purchasing a small van that can meet federal requirements for carpooling. You will obviously sacrifice gas mileage on the vehicle, but you will more than make it up due to the fact that several other vehicles will be in their garages rather than on the road.

35

Boycott Buying

Our final suggestion in this "Shop Green" section is that you specifically avoid certain products. We have already explained how toxins and nonbiodegradable products harm our environment, so we just list some products to avoid completely.

☐ styrofoam

☐ disposable diapers

☐ aerosols: deodorant, hair spray, room freshener, nonfat cooking spray (other convenient forms are available)

☐ nonrechargeable batteries

☐ juice boxes

☐ plastic containers carrying a #7 label (this means that they cannot be recycled)

☐ mercury thermometers

☐ packages that disclose no environmental information.

V

The Garden of Eden

• • • • • • • • • • • • • •

At the beginning of this book we spoke of the Garden of Eden and its significance for us today. We do not repeat that discussion here. We add, simply, that the Creator must delight in plants and animals. Picture God walking through the garden, tending plants, petting animals and showing Adam and Eve the special care he gives to a delicate morning bloom or night crawler. It's more natural for us to care for the garden than we probably know.

We care for the garden for another reason as well: it is linked to our survival. Destruction of God's creation is, in the long run, destruction of what sustains our life. In that sense, environmental concern is the ultimate pro-life issue. We suggest five ways to work the garden.

36
ReLeaf
. . . .

Trees are intimately linked to our survival. One of the
most basic lessons regarding nature—we learn it in elementary
school—is that we exhale carbon dioxide, while trees inhale it.
They in turn exhale oxygen and we inhale it. Our ability to
breathe is interlocked with their ability to breathe.

If you have wondered why all the fuss over the destruction of
the Amazon rain forests, well, this is one of the primary reasons.
The Amazon basin holds the world's largest collection of trees
and essentially is the earth's lungs. Our planet will not survive
without its lungs.

The forests also help protect the planet from extreme heat—
this is part of what is called the "greenhouse effect." Normally,

excess heat generated from our earth and lifestyle escapes into space. But when the trees are destroyed, the heat is absorbed by the abundant carbon dioxide and the atmosphere's temperature rises.

Another way our forests protect the earth is by preventing soil erosion. Millions of tons of good topsoil run off into the oceans every year, stripping the land of its best growing dirt. Several countries in the world today experience famine precisely for this reason.

A final means by which the trees are linked to our survival is rain. Believe it or not, the drought that has regularly ravaged Ethiopia and Sudan over the last decade was caused primarily by the deforestation of the Amazon basin. These gargantuan lungs put moisture back into the air through a process called transpiration, forming rain clouds that are then blown over the ocean by winds and finally "bust loose" in the region of Ethiopia and Sudan. Removing Amazon trees removes Africa's rain supply.

The American Forestry Association has launched the "Global ReLeaf" campaign, perhaps the most successful environmental effort in the history of the world. Entire national governments around the globe have adopted the two-pronged strategy of halting deforestation and *re*foresting areas that have been ravaged by senseless chopping.

We can all help in this ReLeaf effort.

☐ Plant a tree in your yard (consult your local nursery for the best species, method, and position). Consider doing this a couple of times each year.

☐ Talk to local officials about blocking tree cutting in new development projects. Cement suburbs suffer from a quiet deforestation.

☐ Join a town beautification committee, and make it your goal to get trees back to the parks and sidewalks.

☐ Donate funds to the Global ReLeaf campaign every time you donate funds to a hunger relief organization.

☐ Use fewer paper products.

37
ReLeaf at Christmas

· · · · · · · · · · · ·

Christmas rolls around once every year, and part of the national ritual for millions of Americans is to go out and buy a cut tree (or cut their own), put on some Christmas music, stir up the apple cider and decorate the tree.

We don't want to mess with a national ritual, we just want to suggest an adjustment.

Buy a *live* Christmas tree. You will have to pay more for it up front, but in the long run you will have helped save the planet.

Be sure to plan ahead so that you're not caught off guard ten days before Christmas. Sometime in November, talk with your friendly nursery manager. Find out what size tree is most reasonable to cart to your home (root ball and all), and ask to have one put on reserve for you.

Be sure to plan ahead of time what you will do with the tree. Locate (with advice) a spot in your yard where it can thrive and add beauty. If you keep your house cool enough, the tree may survive well in the usual spot inside, covered with ornaments, till Christmas is over and you plant it outdoors. If not, begin a new tradition of planting your Christmas tree when it arrives and decorating it outdoors with weatherproof lights and ornaments.

If your property is large enough, you will be able to create quite a park to mark your care of the environment.

If you live in an apartment and have no yard, well before Christmas you can contact a group that would be interested in taking your live tree after the holidays. Organizations to consider would be the school district, the parks and recreation department and large corporations.

38
A Bird in the . . .
·············

Trees attract birds. The birds "stake out" their terri- tory and build their homes, and their constant singing entertains us while reminding us of the biblical teaching that even if humans stop praising God, the rest of creation certainly will not.

We suggest that you bring birds into your life if they currently are not there. Two good methods are easy for any of us to work on, possibly with the help of a friend or two. If you have kids, let them contribute their creativity to the effort.

Make a Home
Build a birdhouse. These can range from the simple one-room

Motel 6 style to an elaborate Sheraton Hotel arrangement. Pick a model that fits your skill. Your library carries books on building birdhouses. Check them out, and as a family choose your model, purchase the materials and then build the house as a group effort. Research the type of birdseed you need to attract these little flying wonders, so that when your project is complete you will be ready. If possible, have the birdhouse within view of a large window—this way you can enjoy the residents' singing and beauty from indoors.

If you are a little more extravagant, try something a man in Los Angeles did: He hooked up a hummingbird feeder to a rail and pulley that extended from the outdoors into his study. Gradually he moved the feeder indoors, till eventually the hummingbirds just naturally flew into his study for their new round of sweet water.

Bath Time
Another simple project is to build a birdbath. Birds love to splash in water during spring and summer. Again, check out a book and research your options. Possibilities range from a simple stand-alone unit to an elaborate bath that fits into a larger garden motif. Either way, once your project is complete, put out some birdseed to attract the first round of swimmers. Once the word is out you'll have no problem getting more clients.

With a minimum of upkeep required, you've added a family hobby and a set of memories, given yourselves a chance to observe some of God's wonderful creatures up close and (where winter is severe) helped the birds stay alive as food gets scarce.

39

Green Thumb It

• • • • • • • • • • • •

A little gardening can go a long way toward helping us stay close to the miracle of life. The seed dies and is buried, and then it is raised to bloom and bear fruit.

This continual cycle of the earth's giving birth repeats the wonder of creation billions of times over, throughout the world, every day of spring. We recommend that you experiment a little with the life of the earth. Pick a project that suits your lifestyle and limits, because the goal is to enjoy the process and learn. If a certain project seems too big and overwhelming, stay away from it. If you live in an apartment, begin with something as simple as a window planter box.

Don't go it alone. Always remember that friendly nursery manager who wants your business. Explain your goals and you will get all the free advice you need.

Go Organic

As much as possible, experiment with natural care of the earth instead of using chemicals. Your nursery can help you make that start. Read nursery ads in your newspaper if you live in a large town. Some nurseries specialize in organic care. The principle here is to make the soil healthy without introducing toxins that initially give plants a boost but in the long term poison the soil and water system. Pesticides and weed killers are the particular criminals in this regard. Most nurseries can provide you with natural pesticides or put you in touch with a mail-order company that provides them.

Here's your chance to experiment with composting too. If you have a yard, say no to the garbage disposal in your sink. Begin a little compost pile with your grass clippings and vegetable and fruit rinds and cores, and watch your garden grow. Most nurseries have simple guides on how to get your compost going and maintained. It doesn't smell bad; it helps save the planet.

40
*Don't Be
a Dodo*
· · · · · · · · · · · ·

As many as one thousand species are being eliminated from the earth every day. This figure is really beyond our comprehension, but it clearly illustrates to us that the garden is losing inhabitants that can never be replaced.

Unfortunately, the discussion of endangered species has too often been carried out by political extremists who do not talk with each other—they only shout their opinions in the other party's face and by their behavior perpetuate the problem.

Our recommendation is this: Don't be a dodo. Take an interest in the creation and learn from people of differing views. Often the issues related to endangered species are connected to people's livelihood. Consequently, the stakes are high, and the issue appears to be narrowed down to an either-or proposition: the creature's life or mine. The national debate regarding Oregon's spotted owl is a case in point. Logging is a major industry in that region, employing thousands of men and women. People's paychecks are dependent on the freedom to log.

It's important to take an interest in endangered species, because each of them reflects a unique touch of God's creative hand. We should not avoid the subject just because it is surrounded by controversy. Some of the best approaches, we feel, involve simple education. Decide to read one book on endangered species this year. Ask your librarian for a primer. Don't begin with something technical. Next, take an interest in your geographic region. Contact your nearest university to find out what special creation of God (be it plant or animal) indigenous to your area is threatened—and whether there's anything you can do to help save it. Learn and celebrate God's artistry.

You may eventually find yourself drawn into regional issues that seem to pit human well-being against the rest of creation. We encourage you to participate as much as your learning allows, and we urge that your respect for God's creation be matched by your respect of God's character. That is, always conduct yourself in a godly manner that is gentle and humble and that shows high regard for your brothers and sisters, for they are your equals whether or not they agree with your views.

VI

Advocate

• • • • • • • • • • • • • •

Some of you have the special skills and gifts that go with taking a public stand, calling corporations and governments to account for their abuses and pointing to a new or alternative way. Some of you hold positions of influence so that a very small decision on your part can positively impact many people and a large portion of the environment. In this section of the book we are calling for leadership.

We want to stress that all leadership is to be conducted in the spirit of compassion, servanthood, teachability and camaraderie. Stories of environmental advocates who destroy property and endanger the lives of other human beings in order to make their point chill us. That behavior does not reflect a true compassion for creation (humans are the crown of God's creation), nor does it reflect a personal encounter with the personal Creator.

We hope that thousands of our readers will take leadership to stand in the gap, and we offer five ways you can make a difference.

41
Celebrate Earth Day

· · · · · · · · · · · ·

People who are involved in environmental concerns and issues of social justice are often caricatured as being in a bad mood. And that's more accurate than not—unfortunately, the encounter with abuse robs the activist of joy. Yet the *celebration* of God's good creation and character is the real basis for environmental activism.

Earth Day 1991 was a historic event in this regard. Rarely have the peoples of the earth united themselves so completely and enthusiastically around an issue of global importance. That party is over now, and the question is, will we walk away from the issue, not just the party?

Earth Day comes around every April. We suggest you make it

an annual celebration. Here are a few possibilities:

☐ If you are a member of a church or fellowship, arrange well in advance for the Sunday sermon and all Sunday-school lessons, on the Sunday nearest Earth Day, to be centered on the creation and God's call to us to tend the garden.

☐ Work with the local school to sponsor an arts and crafts display by students reflecting their interest in and understanding of environmental concerns. Ask the local mall to display these pieces during Earth Day week.

☐ Put together an all-day concert of local talent on the Saturday nearest Earth Day. Sponsor a plant-a-tree drive to go with the celebration, and party with some good food. *(Clean up* the area after the celebration is over.)

☐ See if your town is willing to decorate Main Street during the two weeks that surround Earth Day, in the same way it decorates for Christmas. This could become an annual event, and the local schools could plan a parade.

42
Educate
· · · · · · · · · · · ·

Most often people are not involved in caring for the environment simply because it all seems too big to grasp. And some feel that our destruction has already gone too far, "so why rearrange the furniture on the deck of the *Titanic?*"

This is where your leadership comes in. Get a feel for the people around you. Try to understand the level at which they have grasped environmental concerns and the aspirations that motivate or fears that block their involvement. Set up educational opportunities accordingly. We recommend the following as possible means toward education:

☐ Sponsor with your local library a half-day seminar on the environment.

☐ Work with your local private and public schools. See if they will let you do a one-hour presentation in each of their classrooms (this could be a year-long commitment).

☐ Approach local churches and fellowship organizations. Offer your services to do a presentation for them in one of their regular educational slots—for example, Friday youth group, Wednesday prayer meeting or Sunday school.

☐ Get the local pastors together and see if they would be interested in a coordinated church effort that would sponsor an all-day seminar on the environment. You could offer to do all the legwork and coordinate the presentations. The cost per participant should be kept to a minimum just to cover materials—say, $4.00 per person, adding another $5.00 if the person wants lunch. Be sure to have several resources on hand for sale, and if the season is right, see if your local nursery will put certain trees and flowers on display, both for educational purposes and for sale.

43

Write the Wrong
......

We mentioned earlier in this book that companies are very sensitive to the consumer. When the green movement made a few flash appearances during the past decade, the business response was "Wait and see." That has changed to the point where businesses now *fear* the anti-green label. We suggest a few ways you can influence companies.

Begin at Home
If you work for a local business, take a couple of lunch hours to do an inventory of the stockroom. Make a list of all the materials bought from corporations unfriendly to the environment. The evidence will be clear enough: Are the products made

from recycled or recyclable materials? If not, research alternative suppliers that can deliver the goods at the same cost, and then approach your supervisors with the data. When changing over to the new suppliers, contact the former suppliers with your reasons. Explain that you will go back to them when they reform their ways.

Go for the Big Hitters

McDonald's could not run and hide. Determined to break down that fast-food chain's intransigence regarding styrofoam, an environmental organization forced it to agree, in a defensive posture, to abandon styrofoam. The pen was used by advocates in two ways.

The McDonald's headquarters was deluged by letters proclaiming a boycott of the chain until behavior changed. That was private but strong enough to get attention.

The same activists began writing letters to the editors of local and national publications, drawing attention to the abuses of McDonald's. Editors picked up on the idea and published strong, well-researched pieces that showed the negative impact McDonald's had on the environment. McDonald's had to change or lose business. It chose to change.

You can do the same. Link up with a couple of friends and make a project out of a supermarket run. Pick three or four products that show absolutely no (or very little) regard for the environment, and then spend an evening together writing letters of protest or concern to the manufacturers. In your letter, list companies that offer the same product or service in an environmentally sound manner. Those to whom you write need to know that an alternative idea works *and* that consumers can make the choice to switch to another available supplier. Write your local newspaper editor, too, and if you have skills in journalism, do a few free-lance pieces on your discoveries.

Send a Good Word

Companies that have made the effort to change need to know that you appreciate their sensitivity. Use all the ideas from the previous suggestions, but in a *positive* frame. Thank these companies for being environmentally responsible and let them know that they have your business. Caring for the environment requires true partnership, and corporations are willing to make necessary changes if they are sure that consumers will put their money where their mouth is.

44
Mark Your "X"
· · · · · · · · · · · ·

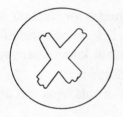

Voting is as all-American as apple pie. Our entire sys-
tem is predicated on the notion that government has no function outside of the will of the people. Citizens who choose not
to influence government through their votes either are very
content with the way things are (and don't sense a change
around the curve) or do not believe that their vote makes a
difference. We are suggesting that both of these positions are
hazardous to the environment.

Influence the government with your knowledge of the issues
and your concern. (To save time, work with several friends, each
of you reading certain reports and publications and then sharing
what you've learned.) There are several levels for involvement,

including the following:

☐ Let local elected officials know that you are watching their performance in light of upcoming elections. Let them know your *specific* concerns.

☐ Do the same at a state and federal level. Congresspersons and senators are vulnerable to your influence. Let them know if you approve or disapprove of their environmental performance, and tell them in specific terms what changes you seek.

☐ Write letters to the editor during election season to address the track record of specific candidates.

☐ Publish leaflets or guides for election week, showing where the different candidates line up on caring for the planet.

☐ Finally, let the president know what you think about his (or maybe one day her) performance.

The resource section of this book has all the appropriate addresses.

45

Make a Scene

· · · · · · · · · · · · ·

Some personality types function well in public confrontation. We need these people, because too many environmental injustices are perpetuated for no other reason than the absence of voices that will clearly and publicly condemn the abuses.

If you live near an environmental abuser and have the personality for protest, seek a meeting with the offending corporation. Make sure you have done your research well so that your presentation is truthfully convincing and helpful. Be gracious but firm. Make it clear that if change does not occur, you will attempt to launch a public protest against the firm. If change is not forthcoming, contact Greenpeace for advice (there you may be able to obtain names and addresses of supporters in your region), and go to it.

Your local churches may also want to lend their voice to the protest. Nothing is as spiritually invigorating and forceful as an all-night candlelight prayer vigil at the gates of an environmental culprit. You may discover the media's support of this approach. Christian groups, unfortunately, are not known for these sensitivities, so it is newsworthy when Christians do show their public commitment to environmental care. Contact the staff of *Sojourners* magazine for materials that could accompany a Christian prayer vigil.

Perhaps you have the funds to influence certain corporations' environmental practices. If so, link up with a few friends to buy shares in an abusive company. Show up at the annual stockholders' meeting and voice your legitimate concerns as a part owner of the corporation. Again, be sure you have done first-class research, and work to present an excellent description of the issues and alternatives involved. Remember, your goal is not to be seen, it's to implement change. You may even discover a very friendly board of directors who will call you into their chambers for a more complete presentation of the issues.

VII

*Resources
for Action*

· · · · · · · · · · · · ·

**What you have in these final pages is a fairly thorough resource
list for activists who want to get a basic library together and
who want to know where to go and whom to contact to make
the environmental voice heard.**

We are convinced that every small step makes a big difference,
so we hope that this resource section encourages you to implement even further the ideas in this book which have caught your
fancy. We offer five categories of resources.

46
Magazines

· · · · · · · · · · · ·

Here are four publications which will help you do your part to save the planet.

ESA Advocate
   A monthly newsletter published by Evangelicals for Social Action. The *Advocate* covers a broad range of social issues, including the environment, from a point of view that is at once biblical and contemporary. $20.00 per year ($15.00 for students). 10 Lancaster Avenue, Philadelphia, PA 19096.

Garbage
   The nation's premier magazine on recycling. Subtitled "The Practical Journal for the Environment." $21.00 per year (six issues). 435 9th Street, Brooklyn, NY 11215.

Greenpeace
   This magazine is the flagship of the international green movement. If you are going to subscribe to only one publication on the environment, *Greenpeace* is our top choice. $30.00 per year (quarterly). 1436 U Street N.W., Washington, DC 20009.

Worldwatch
   Published by the Worldwatch Institute, *Worldwatch* provides in-depth analysis of global situations with a special emphasis on the environment. $20.00 per year (bimonthly). 1776 Massachusetts Avenue N.W., Washington, DC 20036.

47

Books

Look for these titles in your local bookstore. If you don't find the ones you want, ask the store to order them for you.

The Earthworks Group. *50 More Things You Can Do to Save the Earth.* Kansas City, Mo.: Andrews & McMeel, 1991.

———. *50 Simple Things Kids Can Do to Save the Earth.* Kansas City, Mo.: Andrews & McMeel, 1990.

———. *50 Simple Things You Can Do to Save the Earth.* Berkeley: Earth-Works Press, 1989.

———. *50 Simple Things Your Business Can Do to Save the Earth.* Kansas City, Mo.: Andrews & McMeel, 1991.

———. *The Recycler's Handbook.* Berkeley: EarthWorks Press, 1990.

Elkington, John; Julia Hailes and Joel Makower. *The Green Consumer.* New York: Penguin Books, 1990.

Global Tomorrow Coalition. *The Global Ecology Handbook.* Boston: Beacon Press, 1990.

Jansen, Frank Kaleb, ed. *Target Earth.* Pasadena, Calif.: Global Mapping International, 1989.

Ocko, Stephanie. *Environmental Vacations.* Santa Fe, N. M.: John Muir Publications, 1990.

Pederson, Anne. *The Kids' Environment Book.* Santa Fe, N. M.: John Muir Publications, 1991.

48

Federal Agencies and Offices

· · · · · · · · · · ·

Here are some addresses to use either in requesting information or in registering your concerns.

House Agriculture Committee
U.S. House of Representatives
Washington, DC 20515
(202) 225-2171

House Interior Committee
U.S. House of Representatives
Washington, DC 20515
(202) 225-2761

Senate Energy and Natural
  Resources Committee
U.S. Senate
Washington, DC 20510
(202) 224-4971

Department of Agriculture
Soil Conservation Service
14th St. & Independence Ave. S.W.
P.O. Box 2890
Washington, DC 20013
(202) 447-4543

Department of Agriculture
U.S. Forest Service
14th St. & Independence Ave. S.W.
P.O. Box 96090
Washington, DC 20250
(202) 447-2791

Department of Commerce
National Marine Fisheries Service
1335 East-West Highway
Silver Spring, MD 20910
(301) 427-2370

Department of Energy
Federal Energy Regulatory
   Commission
825 N. Capitol St.
Washington, DC 20426
(202) 357-8118

Department of the Interior
Bureau of Land Management
Main Interior Building
18th & C Sts. N.W.
Washington, DC 20240
(202) 343-5717

Department of the Interior
U.S. Fish and Wildlife Service
Main Interior Building
18th & C Sts. N.W.
Washington, DC 20240
(202) 343-5634

Environmental Protection Agency
401 M Street S.W.
Washington, DC 20460
(202) 382-2080

EPA hotlines:
Drinking Water, (800) 426-4791
Pesticides, (800) 585-7378
SARA (Title III) Right-to-Know, (800) 535-0202
Superfund, (202) 382-3000, (800) 424-9346

Write your Senator at
U.S. Senate
Washington, DC 20510

Write your Congressperson at
U.S. House of Representatives
Washington, DC 20515

49

State Recycling Agencies

· · · · · · · · · · · · ·

If recycling hasn't become well established in your community as yet, write to your state agency to request advice and assistance.

Alabama
Department of Environmental
  Management
Solid Waste Branch, Land Division
17151 Congressman Dickinson Dr.
Montgomery, AL 36130
(205) 271-7700

Alaska
Department of Environmental
  Conservation
Recycling
P.O. Box O
Juneau, AK 99811-1800
(907) 465-2671

Arizona
Department of Environmental
  Quality
Waste Planning Section
205 N. Central, 4th Floor
Phoenix, AZ 85004
(602) 257-2372

Department of Commerce
Energy Office
3800 N. Central, Suite 1200
Phoenix, AZ 85012
(800) 352-5499

Arkansas
Pollution Control and Ecology
Solid Waste Management Division
8001 National Drive
Little Rock, AR 72219
(501) 562-7444

California
Department of Conservation
Division of Recycling
1025 P Street
Sacramento, CA 95814
(916) 323-3743
(800) 332-SAVE for your nearest
  recycling center
(800) 642-5669 for information
  on beverage container recycling

Integrated Waste Management
1020 Ninth Street, Suite 300
Sacramento, CA 95814
(916) 322-3330

Colorado
Department of Health
Hazardous Materials and Waste
  Management Division
4210 E. 11th Avenue, Room 351
Denver, CO 80220
(303) 331-4830

Connecticut
Department of Recycling
State Office Building
165 Capitol Avenue
Hartford, CT 06106
(203) 566-8722

Delaware
Department of Natural Resources
  and Environmental Control
Division of Air and Waste
  Management
P.O. Box 1401
89 Kings Highway
Dover, DE 19903
(302) 739-3820

District of Columbia
Office of Recycling
65 K Street, Lower Level
Washington, DC 20002
(202) 939-7116

Florida
Department of Environmental
  Regulation
Division of Waste Management
2600 Blairstone Road
Tallahassee, FL 32399-2400
(904) 488-0300

Georgia
Department of Natural Resources
Environmental Protection Division
3420 Norman Berry Drive,
  7th Floor
Hapeville, GA 30354
(404) 656-2836

Department of Community Affairs
1200 Equitable Building
100 Peachtree Street
Atlanta, GA 30303
(404) 656-3898

Hawaii
Department of Health
Solid and Hazardous Waste
  Division
5 Waterfront Plaza, Suite 250
500 Ala-Moana Blvd.
Honolulu, HI 96813
(808) 543-8227

Idaho
Division of Environmental Quality
IWRAP Bureau
Hazardous Materials Branch
1410 N. Hilton
Boise, ID 83706
(208) 334-5879

Illinois
Office of Solid Waste and
  Renewable Resources
325 W. Adams
Springfield, IL 62704-1892
(217) 524-5454

Indiana
Department of Environmental
  Management
Office of Solid and Hazardous
  Waste Management
105 S. Meridian Street
Indianapolis, IN 46225
(317) 232-8883

Iowa
Department of Natural Resources
Waste Management Authority
  Division
900 E. Grand Avenue
Des Moines, IA 50319
(515) 281-4968

Kansas
Department of Health and
  Environment
Department of Solid Waste
  Management
Building 740, Forbes Field
Topeka, KS 66620
(913) 296-1590

Kentucky
Division of Waste Management
Resources Recovery Branch
18 Reilly Road
Frankfort, KY 40601
(502) 564-6716

Louisiana
Department of Environmental
  Quality
P.O. Box 44096
Baton Rouge, LA 70804-4096
(504) 342-9103

Maine
Waste Management Agency
State House Station #154
Augusta, ME 04333
(207) 289-5300

Maryland
Department of Environmental
 Quality
Hazardous Waste Program
2500 Broening Highway
Building 40, 2nd Floor
Baltimore, MD 21224
(301) 631-3343

Massachusetts
Department of Environmental
 Protection
Division of Solid Waste
 Management
1 Winter Street, 4th Floor
Boston, MA 02108
(617) 292-5980

Michigan
Department of Natural Resources
Waste Management Division
P.O. Box 30241
Lansing, MI 48909
(517) 373-2730

Minnesota
Office of Waste Management
1350 Energy Lane, Suite 201
St. Paul, MN 55108
(612) 649-5750

Pollution Control Agency
520 Lafayette Road
St. Paul, MN 55155
(612) 296-6300

Mississippi
Department of Environmental
 Quality
Office of Pollution Control
P.O. Box 10385
Jackson, MS 39289-0385
(601) 961-5171

Missouri
Department of Natural Resources
P.O. Box 176
Jefferson City, MO 65102
(314) 751-3176

Montana
Department of Health and
 Environmental Science
Solid and Hazardous Waste Bureau
Cogswell Building
Helena, MT 59620
(406) 444-2821

Nebraska
Department of Environmental
 Control
Litter Reduction and Recycling
 Program
P.O. Box 98922
State House Station
Lincoln, NE 68509-8922
(402) 471-2186

Nevada
Office of Community Services
Energy Extension Services
Capitol Complex
Carson City, NV 89710
(702) 687-4908

New Hampshire
Environmental Services
  Department
Waste Management Division
6 Hazen Drive
Concord, NH 03301-6509
(603) 271-2926

New Jersey
Department of Environmental
  Protection
Office of Recycling
850 Bear Tavern Road
Trenton, NJ 08625-0414
(609) 530-4001

New Mexico
Environmental Improvement
  Division
Solid Waste Bureau
Harold Runnels Building
1190 St. Francis Drive
Santa Fe, NM 87503
(505) 827-2959

New York
Department of Environmental
  Conservation
Waste Reduction and Recycling
50 Wolf Road
Albany, NY 12233-4015
(518) 457-7337

North Carolina
Solid Waste Section
P.O. Box 27687
Raleigh, NC 27611-7687
(919) 733-0692

North Dakota
Department of Health
Division of Waste Management
P.O. Box 5520
Bismark, ND 58502-5520
(701) 224-2366

Ohio
Litter Prevention and Recycling
Department of Natural Resources
1889 Fountain Square
Building F-2
Columbus, OH 43224
(614) 265-6353

Oklahoma
Department of Health
Solid Waste Services
P.O. Box 53551
Oklahoma City, OK 73152
(405) 271-7169

Oregon
Department of Environmental
  Quality
Waste Reduction Section
811 S.W. Sixth Avenue, 8th Floor
Portland, OR 97204
(503) 229-5913

Pennsylvania
Department of Environmental
  Resources
Bureau of Waste Management
Waste Reduction/Recycling
P.O. Box 2063
Harrisburg, PA 17105-2063
(717) 787-7382

Rhode Island
Department of Environmental
  Management
O.S.C.A.R.
83 Park Street, 5th Floor
Providence, RI 02903
(401) 277-3434

South Carolina
Bureau of Solid and Hazardous
  Waste
2600 Bull Street
Columbia, SC 29201
(803) 734-5200

South Dakota
Department of Water and Natural
  Resources
Waste Management Program
523 E. Capitol Street
Pierre, SD 57501
(605) 773-3153

Tennessee
Department of Health and
  Environment
Solid Waste Management Division
701 Broadway, 4th Floor,
  Customs House
Nashville, TN 37247-3530
(615) 741-3424

Texas
Department of Health
Division of Solid Waste
  Management
1100 W. 49th Street
Austin, TX 78756
(512) 458-7271

Utah
Department of Environmental
  Health
Solid and Hazardous Waste
P.O. Box 16690
Salt Lake City, UT 84116-0690
(801) 538-6170

Vermont
Department of Environmental
  Conservation
Solid Waste Division
103 S. Main Street, West Building
Waterbury, VT 05676
(802) 244-7831

Virginia
Department of Waste Management
Monroe Building, 11th Floor
101 N. 14th Street
Richmond, VA 23219
(804) 225-2667
Hotline: (800) 552-2075

Washington
Department of Ecology
Recycling Information Office
Eikenberry Building
4407 Woodview Drive S.E.
Lacey, WA 98503
(206) 459-6731
Hotline: (800) RECYCLE

143

West Virginia
Division of Natural Resources
Solid Waste Section
1356 Hansford Street
Charleston, WV 25301
(304) 348-5993

Wisconsin
Department of Natural Resources
Bureau of Solid and Hazardous
  Waste Management
P.O. Box 7921
Madison, WI 53707
(608) 267-7566

Wyoming
Department of Environmental
  Quality
Solid Waste Management
Herschler Building, 4th Floor West
122 W. 25th Street
Cheyenne, WY 82002
(307) 777-7752

50
National
Organizations
. . . .

Each of these groups is concerned for the environment. Write to inquire about their resource materials and programs.

Adopt-A-Stream Foundation
P.O. Box 5558
Everett, WA 98201

African Wildlife Foundation
1717 Massachusetts Avenue N.W.
Washington, DC 20036

American Forestry Association
P.O. Box 2000
Washington, DC 20013

Environmental Defense Fund
257 Park Avenue S.
New York, NY 10010

Global Tomorrow Coalition
1325 G Street N.W.
Washington, DC 20005

Greenpeace
1436 U Street N.W.
Washington, DC 20009

National Geographic Society
17th & M Streets N.W.
Washington, DC 20036

National Wildlife Federation
1400 16th Street N.W.
Washington, DC 20036

Worldwatch Institute
1776 Massachusetts Avenue N.W.
Washington, DC 20036